THIS BOOK BELONGS TO:

_____

_____

NEVER GIVE UP

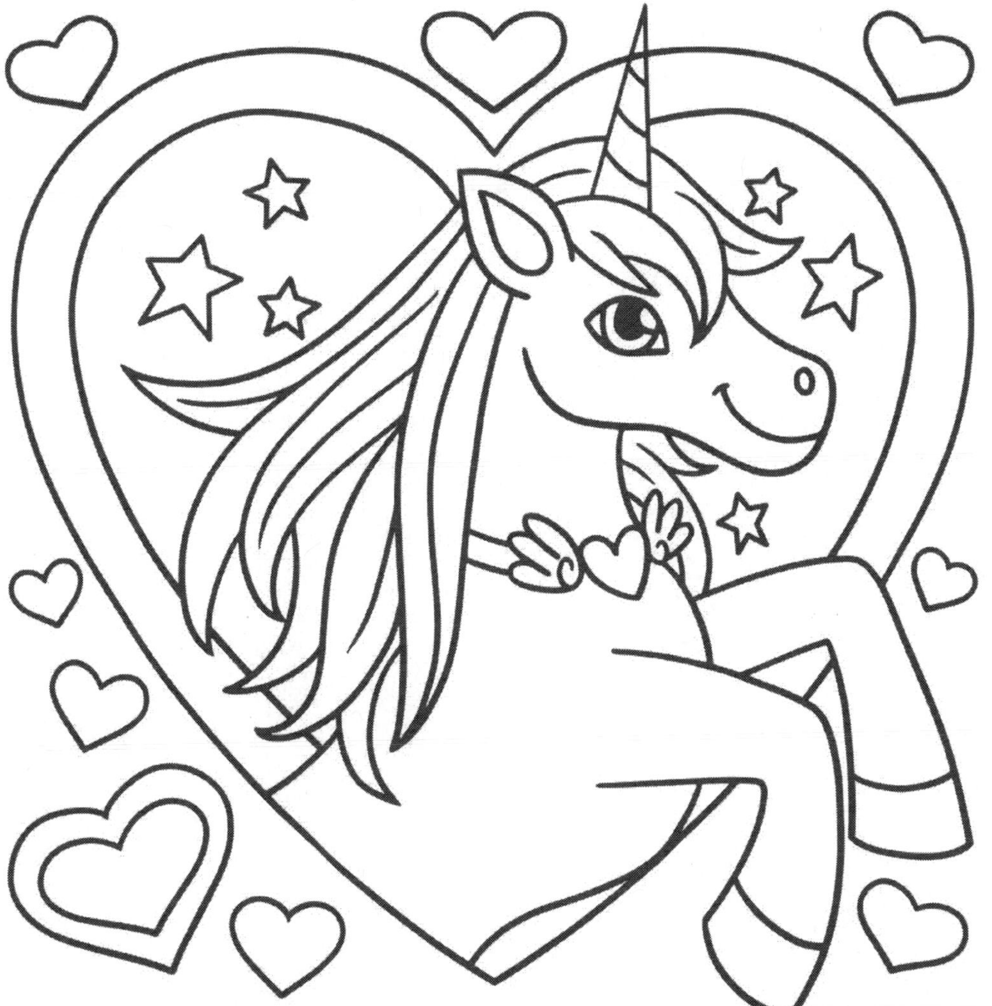

I AM 8 & CONFIDENT

I AM 8 & HAPPY

I AM 8 & WORTHY

Thank you for
purchasing
This book .if you
enjoyed
The feedback on
amazon
Would be greatly
appreciated .

Made in the USA
Las Vegas, NV
08 December 2024

13648978R00083